The Happiness Algorithm

The Happiness Algorithm

Petchinsky

The Happiness Algorithm: Science-Backed Steps to Joyful Living
By: Matthew Petchinsky

Introduction

In a world that often glorifies achievement and external markers of success, happiness remains one of the most elusive pursuits. People chase it relentlessly—through relationships, career milestones, material possessions, and fleeting moments of indulgence. Yet, despite our collective quest, happiness often seems like a mirage, just out of reach. This paradox exists because many of us misunderstand the nature of happiness itself. It is not a destination we arrive at or a reward for ticking off boxes on a checklist. Instead, happiness is a skill—a practice cultivated over time, rooted in sustainable principles of joy that can weather life's inevitable storms.

Why Happiness is a Skill, Not a Destination

Imagine happiness as a garden. It requires deliberate care, consistent effort, and the right conditions to thrive. A garden left unattended will soon be overrun by weeds or parched by neglect. Similarly, happiness flourishes not from one grand act of achievement but from daily actions, habits, and mindsets that nurture our emotional and mental well-being.

The belief that happiness is a destination assumes a linear journey: "Once I achieve this, I'll be happy." This mindset is a trap. It places our well-being in the hands of external circumstances—promotions, relationships, or wealth—that are often beyond our control. Life is unpredictable, and when setbacks occur, this fragile construct of happiness crumbles.

In contrast, viewing happiness as a skill empowers us. Skills can be learned, refined, and adapted over time. They require effort, yes, but they are not dependent on fleeting conditions. Skills like gratitude, mindfulness, emotional resilience, and self-compassion anchor us in the present moment and enable us to find joy even amidst adversity. When happiness becomes a skill, we realize it is not something we "achieve" but something we "practice"—a way of being rather than a place to arrive.

The Principles of Sustainable Joy

To cultivate sustainable joy, we must embrace principles that prioritize internal fulfillment over external validation. Unlike fleeting pleasures, sustainable joy is resilient, enduring, and rooted in practices that align with our values and authentic selves.

1. **Presence and Mindfulness**

   Sustainable joy begins in the present moment. When we dwell in the past or fixate on the future, we rob ourselves of the opportunity to appreciate the here and now. Mindfulness teaches us to savor life's simple pleasures—a warm cup of tea, the laughter of a loved one, or the beauty of a sunset. By being fully present, we deepen our connection to joy.

2. **Gratitude**

   Gratitude is a powerful antidote to dissatisfaction. It shifts our focus from what we lack to what we already have. By cultivating a habit of gratitude—through journaling, reflection, or simply expressing thanks—we rewire our brains to notice the positives in our lives, creating a foundation for lasting happiness.

3. **Resilience in Adversity**

   Life is not without challenges, and sustainable joy does not mean the absence of hardship. Instead, it is the ability to navigate difficulties with grace and resilience. Practices such as reframing negative experiences, seeking support, and focusing on growth help us emerge stronger and more joyful from tough times.

4. **Authenticity and Self-Acceptance**

   True happiness comes from living authentically and embracing ourselves fully—flaws and all. When we let go of societal expectations and pursue what genuinely fulfills us, we create a life aligned with our values, leading to deeper and more sustainable joy.

5. **Connection and Contribution**

   Human beings are wired for connection. Meaningful relationships and acts of kindness not only bring joy to others but also enrich our own lives. By nurturing our connections and contributing to something greater than ourselves, we create a ripple effect of joy that sustains us and those around us.

6. **Growth and Curiosity**

   Joy is not stagnant. It thrives on growth, learning, and exploration. When we challenge ourselves, embrace new experiences, and remain curious, we keep our sense of wonder alive. Growth fuels a deeper sense of purpose, which in turn sustains our happiness.

Conclusion

Happiness is not the end of a journey but the journey itself—a skill we develop, refine, and carry with us through life. It is a mosaic of small, intentional actions that, over time, create a masterpiece of sustainable joy. By embracing happiness as a practice rather than a goal, we liberate ourselves from the endless chase and instead find contentment in the present moment. Through mindfulness, gratitude, resilience, authenticity, connection, and growth, we can cultivate a life not just of fleeting pleasure but of deep, enduring happiness.

As you embark on this journey to master the skill of happiness, remember: the power to create joy lies within you. With commitment and practice, you can transform your life into one of purpose, fulfillment, and lasting contentment.

Chapter 1: Defining Your Joy Blueprint

Happiness is deeply personal, and no two people experience it in the same way. While society often presents a standardized picture of happiness—wealth, success, a picturesque family—it rarely aligns with individual needs and desires. To cultivate authentic and lasting happiness, you must first define what it means to you. This chapter will guide you in understanding your unique vision of happiness and help you create a personalized joy map that serves as your compass in life.

Understanding What Happiness Means to You

Happiness is not a one-size-fits-all concept. What brings joy to one person might leave another feeling empty. For example, some may find happiness in solitude and introspection, while others thrive on social interaction and external stimulation. Understanding your version of happiness requires introspection and honesty.

Reflecting on Your Core Values

Happiness is deeply tied to your core values—the principles and beliefs that matter most to you. When your life aligns with these values, you feel a sense of fulfillment and purpose. Misalignment, on the other hand, creates discontent and frustration.

Take time to identify your core values. Ask yourself:

- What principles guide my decisions?
- When do I feel most at peace with myself?
- What moments in my life have brought me genuine joy, and why?

Some common core values include:

- Freedom
- Creativity
- Family
- Adventure
- Security
- Growth
- Compassion

Once you've identified your values, consider how they currently manifest in your life. Are your actions and goals aligned with them? If not, this could be a source of unhappiness.

Distinguishing Between Internal and External Happiness

It's easy to confuse external markers of happiness—like accolades, possessions, or societal approval—with internal contentment. While external achievements can provide temporary satisfaction, they often fade, leaving you searching for the next "fix."

Internal happiness, however, is sustainable. It stems from self-awareness, gratitude, meaningful relationships, and living in alignment with your values. Recognizing this distinction helps you prioritize what truly matters and avoid chasing superficial goals.

Uncovering Your Joy Triggers

Joy triggers are the activities, experiences, or people that consistently bring you happiness. Reflect on moments when you felt most alive or content. Consider:

- Who were you with?
- What were you doing?
- What feelings were present?

Write these triggers down. Over time, patterns will emerge, offering insights into what truly fuels your happiness.

Creating a Personal Joy Map

A personal joy map is your blueprint for happiness. It's a visual or written representation of your unique pathways to joy, tailored to your values, passions, and aspirations. This map will serve as a practical guide to help you navigate life's complexities while staying grounded in what matters most to you.

Step 1: Identify Your Happiness Anchors

Happiness anchors are the stable elements of your life that provide a foundation for joy. These may include relationships, hobbies, personal achievements, or spiritual practices. To identify your anchors:

1. List the people, activities, and habits that consistently make you feel good.
2. Categorize them into areas such as relationships, health, career, and personal growth.

For example:

- **Relationships**: Spending quality time with family, maintaining deep friendships.
- **Health**: Regular exercise, meditation, healthy eating.
- **Career**: Doing work that aligns with your passions and values.
- **Personal Growth**: Reading, learning new skills, pursuing hobbies.

Step 2: Prioritize Your Goals

Happiness isn't about doing everything at once. It's about focusing on what's most important to you. Look at your happiness anchors and ask:

- Which areas of my life feel neglected?
- What small steps can I take to nurture these areas?

Set realistic, achievable goals that align with your joy blueprint. For instance, if meaningful relationships are a priority, schedule regular time to connect with loved ones.

Step 3: Create a Visual Representation

Translate your joy blueprint into a tangible format. This could be:

- A vision board: Use images, quotes, and symbols that represent your happiness anchors.
- A mind map: Organize your values, goals, and joy triggers into a structured diagram.
- A written plan: Detail your priorities, actionable steps, and long-term aspirations.

The goal is to create something you can revisit regularly to stay inspired and focused.

Step 4: Integrate Your Joy Map into Daily Life

A joy map is only effective if it's used. Integrate its principles into your daily routines by:

- Setting intentions each morning based on your happiness blueprint.
- Reflecting on your progress weekly and making adjustments as needed.
- Celebrating small wins that align with your values and goals.

Overcoming Common Pitfalls

As you define your joy blueprint and create your joy map, you may encounter challenges such as:

1. **External Pressure**: Society, family, or peers may have expectations that conflict with your vision of happiness. Stay true to yourself and remember that your joy blueprint is uniquely yours.
2. **Fear of Change**: Redefining happiness often requires letting go of old habits or goals that no longer serve you. Embrace this change as a necessary step toward fulfillment.
3. **Perfectionism**: Happiness is not about perfection. It's about progress and being kind to yourself along the way.

Conclusion

Defining your joy blueprint is a transformative process that empowers you to take ownership of your happiness. By understanding what happiness truly means to you and creating a personal joy map, you lay the foundation for a life of purpose, fulfillment, and sustainable joy.

As you move forward, keep this blueprint close. Let it guide your decisions, inspire your actions, and remind you that happiness is not something you find—it's something you build, step by step, with intention and care.

Chapter 2: The Happiness Habits

True happiness is not an accidental occurrence but the result of consistent habits and intentional practices. By cultivating rituals for daily contentment and understanding the science behind positive emotions, you can create a life rooted in sustainable joy. In this chapter, we'll explore how to integrate happiness habits into your routine and uncover the fascinating neuroscience behind positive emotions.

Building Rituals for Daily Contentment

Habits are the building blocks of our lives. The small, repetitive actions we perform every day shape not only our routines but also our overall sense of well-being. Happiness habits are rituals designed to foster a sense of contentment and joy in daily life. These practices don't require drastic changes; they thrive on simplicity and consistency.

1. Starting Your Day with Intention

The way you begin your day sets the tone for everything that follows. Incorporate a morning ritual that prioritizes mindfulness, gratitude, or self-care. Some ideas include:

- **Morning Meditation**: Spend 5–10 minutes in silence or guided meditation to center your mind.
- **Gratitude Journaling**: Write down three things you're grateful for every morning.
- **Positive Affirmations**: Repeat empowering statements to boost your confidence and mood.

Starting the day with positivity helps you approach challenges with resilience and clarity.

2. Practicing Mindfulness Throughout the Day

Mindfulness—the practice of being fully present—can significantly enhance daily contentment. Simple ways to incorporate mindfulness include:

- **Mindful Eating**: Pay attention to the taste, texture, and aroma of your food.
- **Focused Breathing**: Pause for a few deep breaths during stressful moments.
- **Nature Walks**: Take a few minutes to observe and appreciate the beauty around you.

These small moments of mindfulness can help you savor life's experiences and reduce stress.

3. Cultivating Gratitude

Gratitude is one of the most powerful happiness habits. It shifts your focus from what's lacking to what you have. Regular gratitude practices can include:

- **Evening Reflection**: End each day by listing three positive moments or things you appreciated.
- **Expressing Thanks**: Verbally thank someone who made your day better.
- **Gratitude Letters**: Write heartfelt letters to people who have positively impacted your life.

Over time, gratitude rewires your brain to naturally seek and notice the good in life.

4. Scheduling Joyful Activities

Happiness thrives when we make time for the things we love. Create rituals around your favorite activities, such as:

- Reading a book or watching a favorite show.
- Engaging in creative hobbies like painting, writing, or gardening.
- Spending quality time with loved ones.

By intentionally carving out time for joy, you prevent the busyness of life from overshadowing your happiness.

5. Building Resilience Through Self-Compassion

Self-compassion—treating yourself with kindness during difficult times—is a critical happiness habit. Cultivate it through practices like:

- Speaking to yourself as you would a close friend.
- Recognizing that struggles are a normal part of the human experience.
- Giving yourself permission to rest and recharge when needed.

Self-compassion builds emotional resilience, helping you navigate challenges with grace.

The Neuroscience of Positive Emotions

Happiness is not just a feeling; it's a biological phenomenon rooted in the brain. Understanding the neuroscience behind positive emotions can help you cultivate practices that boost your happiness on a neurological level.

The Role of Neurotransmitters

Positive emotions are primarily influenced by specific neurotransmitters—chemical messengers in the brain. The key players include:

1. **Dopamine**
   - Known as the "reward chemical," dopamine is released when you achieve a goal or experience something pleasurable.
   - Activities that boost dopamine: setting and completing small tasks, listening to music, or engaging in creative pursuits.

2. **Serotonin**
   - Often called the "mood stabilizer," serotonin regulates mood and contributes to feelings of well-being.
   - Activities that boost serotonin: exposure to sunlight, exercise, and practicing gratitude.

3. **Oxytocin**
   - Referred to as the "love hormone," oxytocin fosters connection and trust in relationships.
   - Activities that boost oxytocin: hugging, spending time with loved ones, or acts of kindness.

4. **Endorphins**
   - These are the body's natural painkillers, released during exercise or laughter. They create a sense of euphoria.
   - Activities that boost endorphins: exercising, laughing, or engaging in activities you enjoy.

The Brain's Happiness Centers

The brain's architecture includes regions that play a significant role in generating positive emotions:

- **Prefrontal Cortex**: Associated with decision-making and emotional regulation, this area helps you focus on positive experiences.
- **Amygdala**: While often linked to fear, the amygdala also processes positive emotions when activated by joyful experiences.
- **Nucleus Accumbens**: A key part of the brain's reward system, it processes pleasure and motivation.

Understanding these regions can help you design habits that stimulate the brain's happiness centers.

The Power of Neuroplasticity

One of the most exciting aspects of neuroscience is neuroplasticity—the brain's ability to adapt and change throughout life. Positive habits can strengthen neural pathways associated with happiness, making joy more accessible over time.

For example, regularly practicing gratitude increases activity in the prefrontal cortex, while mindfulness enhances the brain's ability to regulate emotions.

Building a Happiness Habit Framework

To effectively integrate happiness habits into your life, follow these steps:

1. **Start Small**

   Begin with one or two habits that feel manageable. Small, consistent changes are more sustainable than drastic overhauls.

2. **Use Triggers**

   Pair new habits with existing routines. For example, practice gratitude while brushing your teeth or take a few deep breaths before meals.

3. **Track Your Progress**

   Keep a journal or use an app to monitor your habits. Reflecting on your progress reinforces commitment and provides motivation.

4. **Celebrate Wins**

   Acknowledge and reward yourself for sticking to your habits. Positive reinforcement strengthens your motivation.

5. **Adapt and Evolve**

   Life is dynamic, and so are your needs. Reassess your happiness habits periodically and make adjustments as needed.

Conclusion

Happiness is a skill, and like any skill, it requires practice. By building rituals for daily contentment and leveraging the neuroscience of positive emotions, you can create a life rich in joy and resilience.

These habits are not quick fixes but lifelong practices that grow stronger with time. As you continue to integrate them into your routine, you'll find that happiness becomes less about fleeting moments and more about a steady, enduring presence in your life.

The journey to happiness starts with small, intentional steps. Begin today, and watch as these practices transform your daily experience into one of fulfillment and joy.

Chapter 3: Connection and Community

Humans are inherently social beings. While personal growth and self-awareness are integral to happiness, the role of connection and community cannot be overstated. Relationships—whether with family, friends, colleagues, or communities—serve as the foundation of emotional well-being. In this chapter, we will explore how to strengthen relationships to enhance happiness and delve into the profound impact of social support on overall well-being.

Strengthening Relationships for Happiness

Healthy, meaningful relationships are a cornerstone of happiness. They provide a sense of belonging, emotional support, and shared joy. However, maintaining strong relationships requires effort, communication, and intentionality.

1. The Foundation of Strong Relationships

Strong relationships are built on trust, respect, and mutual understanding. Key elements include:

- **Empathy**: The ability to understand and share the feelings of another person fosters deep connections. Practice active listening and validate others' emotions to build trust.
- **Communication**: Honest and open communication is essential. Share your thoughts, feelings, and needs while also being receptive to those of others.
- **Boundaries**: Healthy relationships respect individual boundaries. Be clear about your limits and honor the boundaries of others.

2. Practicing Gratitude in Relationships

Expressing gratitude strengthens bonds and creates positive interactions. A simple "thank you" can go a long way in showing appreciation. Consider:

- Writing thank-you notes for acts of kindness.
- Verbally acknowledging the positive traits of those around you.
- Reflecting on what you value most in your relationships.

Gratitude not only uplifts others but also enhances your sense of connection and joy.

3. Creating Rituals of Connection

Consistency in relationships fosters trust and deepens bonds. Establish rituals that prioritize connection, such as:

- Weekly family dinners or game nights.
- Regular calls or check-ins with distant friends.
- Celebrating milestones or achievements together.

These rituals provide opportunities for meaningful interaction and reinforce the importance of your relationships.

4. Navigating Conflict with Compassion

Conflict is inevitable in any relationship, but it doesn't have to be destructive. Approaching disagreements with compassion and a willingness to understand strengthens bonds. Consider:

- Using "I" statements to express feelings without blame.
- Seeking to understand the other person's perspective.
- Taking a break if emotions run high, then returning to the discussion calmly.

By resolving conflicts constructively, you build resilience and trust within your relationships.

5. Investing in Quality Over Quantity

It's not the number of relationships you have but the quality of those connections that matters most. Focus on nurturing a few deep, meaningful relationships rather than spreading yourself thin across many superficial ones.

The Impact of Social Support on Well-Being

Social support is more than a comfort during difficult times; it is a critical determinant of mental and physical health. Studies consistently show that strong social networks contribute to longer life spans, reduced stress levels, and greater happiness.

1. Types of Social Support

Social support comes in various forms, each playing a unique role in well-being:

- **Emotional Support**: Providing empathy, love, and care during times of need.
- **Instrumental Support**: Offering tangible assistance, such as help with tasks or financial aid.
- **Informational Support**: Sharing advice, guidance, or resources.
- **Companionship**: Simply being present and spending time together.

Each type of support contributes to a sense of security and belonging.

2. The Biological Benefits of Social Support

Social connections have measurable effects on the body:

- **Stress Reduction**: Interacting with supportive individuals lowers cortisol levels, reducing stress.
- **Improved Heart Health**: Close relationships are linked to lower blood pressure and a reduced risk of cardiovascular disease.
- **Enhanced Immunity**: People with strong social networks have better immune function, making them more resilient to illness.
- **Increased Longevity**: Studies reveal that individuals with robust social ties live longer, healthier lives.

These benefits highlight the profound influence of relationships on physical well-being.

3. Social Support and Mental Health

Strong social support systems are a protective factor against mental health challenges. They:

- Decrease the risk of depression and anxiety.
- Provide a sense of purpose and meaning.
- Offer a buffer against the effects of trauma or adversity.

Knowing that someone cares about you and has your back is one of the most powerful contributors to emotional resilience.

4. Building and Expanding Your Support Network

If your social network feels limited, take proactive steps to build connections:

- **Join Groups or Communities**: Participate in local clubs, classes, or volunteer organizations. Shared interests create natural opportunities for connection.
- **Reconnect with Old Friends**: Reach out to people you've lost touch with to rekindle meaningful relationships.
- **Be Open to New Connections**: Approach new acquaintances with curiosity and kindness. You never know where a conversation might lead.

Expanding your support network takes time but is worth the effort for the long-term benefits to your well-being.

Strengthening Community Ties

While close personal relationships are essential, community connections also play a vital role in happiness. Being part of a community fosters a sense of belonging and shared purpose.

1. Contributing to Your Community

Acts of contribution not only benefit others but also enhance your own happiness. Consider:

- Volunteering for causes you care about.
- Supporting local businesses or initiatives.
- Participating in community events or gatherings.

When you contribute to something larger than yourself, you experience a sense of fulfillment and connection.

2. Finding Your Tribe

Communities can be based on shared interests, values, or experiences. Whether it's a book club, religious group, or online forum, finding your tribe creates a network of support and camaraderie.

3. Embracing Diversity

Connecting with individuals from diverse backgrounds enriches your perspective and deepens your empathy. Embrace opportunities to learn from others' experiences and broaden your social circle.

Overcoming Barriers to Connection

Modern life often presents challenges to building and maintaining relationships:

1. **Technology Overuse**: While technology can facilitate connection, excessive screen time can also hinder meaningful interaction. Be intentional about balancing online and offline connections.
2. **Fear of Vulnerability**: Opening up to others can feel risky, but vulnerability is the gateway to deep, authentic relationships. Start small and build trust gradually.
3. **Busy Schedules**: Prioritize relationships by scheduling time for connection, just as you would for work or other responsibilities.

Conclusion

Connection and community are essential ingredients for a happy and fulfilling life. By strengthening your relationships and fostering social support, you create a robust foundation for emotional and physical well-being.

Happiness is not a solitary journey—it thrives in the presence of others. As you nurture your connections and contribute to your community, you'll discover that the joy of shared experiences far outweighs the fleeting pleasures of isolation. Embrace the power of connection, and watch as your life becomes richer, more meaningful, and profoundly joyful.

Chapter 4: Growth Through Gratitude

Gratitude is often described as the gateway to joy. It's more than a polite "thank you" or fleeting acknowledgment; it's a transformative practice that rewires the way we perceive our lives. Gratitude amplifies our joy by shifting focus from what we lack to the abundance already present. Additionally, gratitude plays a crucial role in transforming setbacks into opportunities for growth, helping us navigate life's challenges with resilience and optimism.

Practicing Gratitude for Amplified Joy

Gratitude is not just a feeling but a habit—a deliberate choice to see and appreciate the positives in life. When cultivated consistently, it elevates happiness, fosters contentment, and strengthens emotional resilience.

1. The Science of Gratitude

Gratitude has profound effects on both the mind and body. Research in positive psychology reveals that practicing gratitude can:

- **Boost Mental Health**: Gratitude reduces symptoms of depression and anxiety, enhancing overall well-being.
- **Enhance Relationships**: Expressing gratitude strengthens bonds and fosters deeper connections with others.
- **Improve Physical Health**: Studies show that grateful individuals have better sleep quality, lower blood pressure, and stronger immune systems.
- **Increase Happiness Levels**: Gratitude activates brain regions associated with reward and contentment, amplifying joy over time.

The consistent practice of gratitude creates a positive feedback loop, where noticing the good in life leads to greater feelings of joy, which in turn makes it easier to recognize even more blessings.

2. Building a Gratitude Practice

Incorporating gratitude into daily life doesn't require grand gestures. Simple, consistent practices can yield profound results.

- **Gratitude Journaling**: Spend a few minutes each day writing down three things you're grateful for. Be specific and reflect on why these things matter to you.
- **Daily Gratitude Affirmations**: Begin your day with positive statements such as, "I am grateful for the opportunities this day will bring."
- **Gratitude Walks**: Take a walk and consciously notice the beauty around you—nature, architecture, or the kindness of strangers.
- **Sharing Gratitude**: Verbally express your appreciation to someone who has positively impacted your life.

3. Cultivating Gratitude in Difficult Moments

Gratitude is most powerful when practiced during challenging times. Instead of denying difficulties, gratitude helps reframe them. For example:

- Reflect on what the experience is teaching you.
- Identify support or resources you can lean on during hardship.
- Focus on small comforts or blessings that bring relief, even in the face of struggle.

By shifting your perspective, gratitude transforms adversity into an opportunity to grow.

Turning Setbacks into Growth Opportunities

Life is inevitably filled with setbacks, failures, and disappointments. While these moments can be painful, they also hold the potential for profound growth. Gratitude serves as a bridge between hardship and personal transformation, enabling you to find meaning and resilience in the face of adversity.

1. Reframing Challenges with Gratitude

When faced with setbacks, the natural reaction is often frustration, anger, or despair. However, gratitude provides a lens through which challenges can be viewed as opportunities for growth. Consider:

- **What Can I Learn?** Setbacks often highlight areas for improvement or growth. For example, a failed project may teach you valuable lessons about preparation, teamwork, or adaptability.
- **Who or What Has Supported Me?** Even during hardship, there are often people, resources, or circumstances that provide support or relief. Recognizing these elements fosters gratitude.
- **How Has This Made Me Stronger?** Overcoming challenges builds resilience, confidence, and inner strength, equipping you for future difficulties.

2. Practicing Post-Traumatic Growth

Post-traumatic growth refers to the positive transformation that can occur after experiencing adversity. Key areas of growth include:

- **Greater Appreciation for Life**: Difficulties often sharpen your awareness of life's fleeting and precious nature.
- **Improved Relationships**: Adversity can strengthen bonds with those who support you during tough times.
- **Increased Resilience**: Surviving hardship builds mental toughness and resourcefulness.

Gratitude plays a critical role in facilitating this growth by helping you focus on the positive aspects of your recovery journey.

3. Using Gratitude to Build a Growth Mindset

A growth mindset—the belief that abilities and intelligence can be developed through effort—is essential for turning setbacks into stepping stones. Gratitude reinforces a growth mindset by shifting the narrative from "Why me?" to "What can I learn?" or "How can I grow?"

To foster a growth mindset:

- View failures as temporary and specific, rather than permanent and personal.
- Celebrate effort and progress, even if the outcome wasn't ideal.
- Use gratitude to acknowledge the lessons learned and the strength gained.

4. Strategies for Gratitude During Setbacks

While gratitude may not come naturally during challenging times, specific strategies can help cultivate it:

- **Keep a "Resilience Journal"**: Document what you're learning from setbacks and the ways you're growing stronger.
- **Seek Perspective**: Compare your current challenge to past hardships you've overcome, and recognize your capacity to endure.
- **Find the Silver Linings**: Actively look for any positive outcomes or opportunities hidden within the difficulty.

Gratitude as a Tool for Empowerment

Gratitude empowers you to take control of your narrative, even when circumstances feel overwhelming. It shifts focus from what is outside your control to what you can influence—your perspective, attitude, and actions.

1. Strengthening Emotional Resilience

Gratitude fosters emotional resilience by:

- Helping you bounce back more quickly from adversity.
- Reducing stress and anxiety by redirecting attention to the positives in your life.
- Encouraging hope and optimism for the future.

2. Building Deeper Connections

Gratitude strengthens relationships by fostering a sense of mutual appreciation and support. Expressing gratitude regularly creates a positive feedback loop, where others feel valued and are more likely to reciprocate kindness and support.

3. Increasing Self-Worth

Practicing gratitude includes recognizing your own contributions and strengths. For example, instead of focusing solely on external validation, reflect on your personal growth, achievements, and the qualities you bring to your relationships and endeavors.

The Lifelong Practice of Gratitude

Gratitude is not a one-time fix but a lifelong practice. Its benefits compound over time, deepening your joy and resilience. To sustain this practice:

- Set aside time each day for gratitude reflections, no matter how small.
- Surround yourself with reminders of what you're grateful for, such as photos, affirmations, or mementos.

- Share your gratitude journey with others to inspire and strengthen your collective well-being.

Conclusion

Gratitude is a transformative force that amplifies joy, fosters resilience, and turns life's challenges into opportunities for growth. By integrating gratitude into your daily life, you not only elevate your own happiness but also create a ripple effect of positivity that touches those around you.

Setbacks, when viewed through the lens of gratitude, lose their sting and become catalysts for personal evolution. As you continue to cultivate this powerful habit, you'll discover that gratitude is not just an emotion—it's a way of life that paves the path to enduring happiness and growth.

Chapter 5: Designing a Life You Love

A life you love is not one built by accident but through intentional choices, meaningful goals, and a mindset that embraces joy in every step of the journey. While society often emphasizes outcomes—achievements, milestones, and accolades—it is the alignment of your daily actions with your core values and the ability to find joy in the process that create a truly fulfilling life. In this chapter, we'll explore how to align your goals with your happiness and embrace the journey, rather than merely focusing on the destination.

Aligning Goals with Happiness

Goals provide direction and purpose, but not all goals contribute to happiness. To design a life you love, your goals must align with your values, passions, and authentic self.

1. The Importance of Value-Driven Goals

Value-driven goals are those that reflect what matters most to you. They align with your inner priorities rather than external pressures or societal expectations.

To identify value-driven goals:

- **Clarify Your Core Values**: Reflect on principles like creativity, family, adventure, security, or personal growth.
- **Evaluate Your Current Goals**: Ask yourself if your goals align with your values. For example, if family is a core value but work dominates your time, reassess your priorities.
- **Set Meaningful Objectives**: Choose goals that bring a sense of purpose and fulfillment, rather than simply ticking off boxes or pleasing others.

2. Setting Goals that Promote Happiness

When setting goals, focus on those that enhance well-being and joy. Consider:

- **Intrinsic vs. Extrinsic Goals**: Intrinsic goals, like self-improvement or helping others, lead to greater happiness than extrinsic goals, like wealth or status.
- **Process-Oriented Goals**: Goals that emphasize growth and effort, such as learning a new skill, are more fulfilling than purely result-driven goals.
- **Balance**: Include goals across different areas of life—relationships, health, personal growth, and leisure—to ensure a well-rounded sense of happiness.

3. Breaking Goals into Achievable Steps

Overly ambitious goals can lead to stress and burnout. To maintain joy, break larger goals into smaller, manageable steps. For example:

- Instead of "Write a book," focus on "Write 500 words daily."
- Instead of "Run a marathon," aim for "Run 3 miles three times a week."

Small, consistent progress builds momentum and keeps you motivated while allowing you to celebrate incremental successes.

4. Avoiding the Trap of Misaligned Goals

Sometimes, we pursue goals that we think will bring happiness but instead create stress or dissatisfaction. Common misalignments include:

- Chasing goals imposed by others or society, rather than your own desires.
- Pursuing success at the expense of relationships or health.
- Focusing on short-term gains that conflict with long-term values.

Regularly reassess your goals to ensure they remain aligned with your evolving priorities and values.

Finding Joy in the Process, Not Just the Outcome

Happiness is not a destination but a journey. When you focus solely on outcomes, you risk missing the joy inherent in the process. Embracing the journey requires a mindset shift that values growth, effort, and the experiences along the way.

1. The Danger of Outcome-Based Thinking

Outcome-based thinking places all emphasis on the end goal, such as landing a promotion, losing weight, or earning a degree. While achieving these goals can bring satisfaction, the happiness is often short-lived. Common pitfalls include:

- **Post-Goal Letdown**: Feeling empty or aimless after achieving a major milestone.
- **Perfectionism**: Placing unrealistic pressure on yourself to meet high standards, leading to stress and disappointment.
- **Neglecting the Present**: Becoming so focused on the future that you miss out on the joy of the present moment.

2. Cultivating a Process-Oriented Mindset

To find joy in the process, shift your focus from results to the journey itself. Strategies include:

- **Practice Presence**: Engage fully in each step of the process, whether it's brainstorming ideas, learning new skills, or solving challenges.
- **Celebrate Small Wins**: Acknowledge and appreciate each milestone, no matter how small. This reinforces progress and motivation.
- **Reframe Setbacks**: View mistakes or delays as opportunities for growth and learning, rather than failures.

3. Infusing Joy into Daily Tasks

Even mundane or challenging tasks can be made more enjoyable with intentional effort. Consider:

- **Adding Elements of Fun**: Listen to music while working, or turn chores into a game.
- **Creating Rituals**: Establish meaningful rituals around tasks, such as a morning coffee routine while planning your day.
- **Finding Purpose**: Connect each task to a larger purpose. For example, see a workout as part of a commitment to health, or view studying as a step toward personal growth.

4. Embracing Growth and Transformation

The journey toward your goals is often where the most significant personal growth occurs. Reflect on:

- **How You've Grown**: Consider the skills, insights, or relationships gained along the way.
- **The Value of Effort**: Recognize that effort itself is rewarding, as it builds resilience, discipline, and confidence.
- **The Unpredictable Joys**: Be open to unexpected discoveries or connections that arise during the process.

Creating a Life Design Plan

Designing a life you love involves weaving together aligned goals and a process-oriented mindset into a cohesive plan.

1. Visualizing Your Ideal Life

Imagine your ideal life in detail. Consider:

- What does a joyful day look like for you?
- How do you spend your time, and who do you spend it with?
- What values, passions, or goals are central to your life?

Use this vision as a guiding star for your decisions and priorities.

2. Designing Your Days with Intention

Your daily habits shape your life over time. To align your actions with your goals and values:

- **Create a Morning Routine**: Start each day with practices that set a positive tone, such as meditation, journaling, or exercise.
- **Batch Activities**: Group similar tasks together to maximize efficiency and free up time for meaningful pursuits.
- **Reflect and Adjust**: End each day with a brief reflection on what went well and what could improve, then adjust your plan as needed.

3. Embracing Flexibility

Life is unpredictable, and rigid plans can create unnecessary stress. Build flexibility into your life design by:

- Allowing space for spontaneity and new opportunities.
- Adapting your goals as circumstances change.

- Practicing self-compassion when things don't go as planned.

Conclusion

Designing a life you love is an ongoing process that requires self-awareness, intentionality, and a willingness to embrace the present moment. By aligning your goals with your core values and finding joy in the journey, you create a life rich in meaning, fulfillment, and sustainable happiness.

The journey to happiness isn't about reaching a final destination but about cultivating a life that reflects who you truly are. Embrace the process, celebrate your growth, and savor the moments that make the journey worthwhile. In doing so, you'll discover that a life you love isn't something you wait for—it's something you build every single day.

Appendix A: Gratitude Journal Template

A gratitude journal is a powerful tool for cultivating happiness and mindfulness. By setting aside a few minutes each day to reflect on what you're grateful for, you can reframe your perspective, enhance your mood, and build a habit that supports long-term well-being. The following template provides structure and inspiration to help you create your own gratitude journal practice.

Gratitude Journal Overview

Frequency: Daily (or as often as possible)

Time Required: 5–15 minutes

Materials Needed: Notebook or journal, pen, or a digital journaling app

Tips for Effective Gratitude Journaling:

1. Be specific: Instead of writing "I'm grateful for my friends," try "I'm grateful for the phone call with my friend Sarah today, which made me feel supported."
2. Focus on variety: Avoid repeating the same entries each day to keep your practice fresh and engaging.
3. Reflect on the "why": Think about why you're grateful for each item to deepen the impact of your reflection.
4. Include challenges: Consider what lessons or growth opportunities you're grateful for, even from difficult experiences.

Daily Gratitude Journal Template
1. Date and Mood Check-In

- **Date:** Write today's date.
- **Mood:** On a scale of 1 to 10 (1 being very low, 10 being very high), rate your current mood. Optionally, include a brief description of how you're feeling (e.g., "Excited and hopeful" or "Tired but content").

2. Three Things I'm Grateful For
Write three specific things you are grateful for today. Use the prompts below if you need inspiration:

- A person who made a positive impact on your day.
- An accomplishment or small win.
- A moment that brought you joy or peace.
- Something in nature that caught your attention.
- A skill or quality you appreciate about yourself.

Example:

1. The sunny weather that made my walk enjoyable.
2. My coworker helping me with a challenging project.
3. Finding time to read a chapter of my favorite book.

3. Gratitude Reflection (Optional)
Choose one of the items from your list above and expand on it:

- **Why are you grateful for it?**
- **How did it make you feel?**
- **What impact did it have on your day?**

Example:

"I'm grateful for my coworker helping me with a challenging project. It reminded me that I'm part of a supportive team, and it made a task that felt overwhelming manageable. It also deepened my appreciation for collaboration."

4. Gratitude for Challenges

Reflect on a challenge you're currently facing and identify one aspect you're grateful for:

- What lesson is this challenge teaching you?
- What strengths are you developing as a result?

Example:

"I'm facing a tight deadline at work, but I'm grateful because it's teaching me better time management and helping me prioritize tasks more effectively."

5. Intention for Tomorrow

Set a positive intention for the next day based on your gratitude reflections. This intention can guide your mindset and actions.

Example:

"Tomorrow, I will express gratitude to my coworker who helped me today by sending them a thank-you note."

Weekly Gratitude Summary (Optional)

At the end of each week, reflect on your gratitude entries to identify patterns or recurring themes. Use the prompts below to summarize your gratitude practice:

- What were the top three things you were grateful for this week?
- Did any particular people, moments, or experiences stand out?
- How did practicing gratitude impact your mood or perspective?
- What goals or intentions can you set for the coming week to build on this gratitude?

Example:

"This week, I was most grateful for my supportive coworkers, quality time with my family, and the chance to explore a new hiking trail. Practicing gratitude helped me feel more connected and optimistic. Next week, I will focus on expressing gratitude to those who've supported me and finding joy in small daily moments."

Additional Prompts for Deepening Gratitude

If you want to explore gratitude more deeply or vary your entries, try the following prompts:

1. Who has inspired you recently, and why?
2. What is a small luxury or comfort you often take for granted?
3. What past experience are you grateful for, and how has it shaped you?
4. What is a recent kindness someone showed you?
5. What is something about your health or body that you appreciate?

Gratitude Journal Printable Pages
Daily Entry Template:

Date: **Mood (1–10):**

Three Things I'm Grateful For:
Reflection on One Item:
Gratitude for Challenges:
Intention for Tomorrow:
By using this template, you can establish a consistent and meaningful gratitude practice that fosters joy, resilience, and a positive outlook on life. Remember, the beauty of a gratitude journal lies in its simplicity and adaptability. Feel free to customize it to fit your needs and preferences.

Message from the Author:

I hope you enjoyed this book, I love astrology and knew there was not a book such as this out on the shelf. I love metaphysical items as well. Please check out my other books:

-Life of Government Benefits

-My life of Hell

-My life with Hydrocephalus

-Red Sky

-World Domination:Woman's rule

-World Domination:Woman's Rule 2: The War

-Life and Banishment of Apophis: book 1

-The Kidney Friendly Diet

-The Ultimate Hemp Cookbook

-Creating a Dispensary(legally)

-Cleanliness throughout life: the importance of showering from childhood to adulthood.

-Strong Roots: The Risks of Overcoddling children

-Hemp Horoscopes: Cosmic Insights and Earthly Healing

- Celestial Hemp Navigating the Zodiac: Through the Green Cosmos

-Astrological Hemp: Aligning The Stars with Earth's Ancient Herb

-The Astrological Guide to Hemp: Stars, Signs, and Sacred Leaves

-Green Growth: Innovative Marketing Strategies for your Hemp Products and Dispensary

-Cosmic Cannabis

-Astrological Munchies

-Henry The Hemp

-Zodiacal Roots: The Astrological Soul Of Hemp

- **Green Constellations: Intersection of Hemp and Zodiac**

-Hemp in The Houses: An astrological Adventure Through The Cannabis Galaxy

-Galactic Ganja Guide

Heavenly Hemp

Zodiac Leaves

Doctor Who Astrology

Cannastrology

Stellar Satvias and Cosmic Indicas

Celestial Cannabis: A Zodiac Journey

AstroHerbology: The Sky and The Soil: Volume 1

AstroHerbology:Celestial Cannabis:Volume 2

Cosmic Cannabis Cultivation

The Starry Guide to Herbal Harmony: Volume 1

The Starry Guide to Herbal Harmony: Cannabis Universe: Volume 2

Yugioh Astrology: Astrological Guide to Deck, Duels and more

Nightmare Mansion: Echoes of The Abyss

Nightmare Mansion 2: Legacy of Shadows

Nightmare Mansion 3: Shadows of the Forgotten

Nightmare Mansion 4: Echoes of the Damned

The Life and Banishment of Apophis: Book 2

Nightmare Mansion: Halls of Despair

Healing with Herb: Cannabis and Hydrocephalus

Planetary Pot: Aligning with Astrological Herbs: Volume 1

Fast Track to Freedom: 30 Days to Financial Independence Using AI, Assets, and Agile Hustles

Cosmic Hemp Pathways

How to Become Financially Free in 30 Days: 10,000 Paths to Prosperity

Zodiacal Herbage: Astrological Insights: Volume 1

Nightmare Mansion: Whispers in the Walls

The Daleks Invade Atlantis

Henry the hemp and Hydrocephalus

10X The Kidney Friendly Diet

Cannabis Universe: Adult coloring book

Hemp Astrology: The Healing Power of the Stars

Zodiacal Herbage: Astrological Insights: Cannabis Universe: Volume 2

<u>Planetary Pot: Aligning with Astrological Herbs: Cannabis Universes: Volume 2</u>

Doctor Who Meets the Replicators and SG-1: The Ultimate Battle for Survival

Nightmare Mansion: Curse of the Blood Moon

<u>The Celestial Stoner: A Guide to the Zodiac</u>

Cosmic Pleasures: Sex Toy Astrology for Every Sign

Hydrocephalus Astrology: Navigating the Stars and Healing Waters

Lapis and the Mischievous Chocolate Bar

Celestial Positions: Sexual Astrology for Every Sign

Apophis's Shadow Work Journal: : A Journey of Self-Discovery and Healing

Kinky Cosmos: Sexual Kink Astrology for Every Sign

Digital Cosmos: The Astrological Digimon Compendium

Stellar Seeds: The Cosmic Guide to Growing with Astrology

Apophis's Daily Gratitude Journal

Cat Astrology: Feline Mysteries of the Cosmos

The Cosmic Kama Sutra: An Astrological Guide to Sexual Positions

Unleash Your Potential: A Guided Journal Powered by AI Insights

Whispers of the Enchanted Grove

Cosmic Pleasures: An Astrological Guide to Sexual Kinks

369, 12 Manifestation Journal

Whisper of the nocturne journal(blank journal for writing or drawing)

The Boogey Book

Locked In Reflection: A Chastity Journey Through Locktober

Generating Wealth Quickly:

How to Generate $100,000 in 24 Hours

Star Magic: Harness the Power of the Universe

The Flatulence Chronicles: A Fart Journal for Self-Discovery

The Doctor and The Death Moth

Seize the Day: A Personal Seizure Tracking Journal

The Ultimate Boogeyman Safari: A Journey into the Boogie World and Beyond

Whispers of Samhain: 1,000 Spells of Love, Luck, and Lunar Magic: Samhain Spell Book

Apophis's guides:

Witch's Spellbook Crafting Guide for Halloween

<u>Frost & Flame: The Enchanted Yule Grimoire of 1000 Winter Spells</u>

<u>The Ultimate Boogey Goo Guide & Spooky Activities for Halloween Fun</u>

Harmony of the Scales: A Libra's Spellcraft for Balance and Beauty

The Enchanted Advent: 36 Days of Christmas Wonders

Nightmare Mansion: The Labyrinth of Screams

Harvest of Enchantment: 1,000 Spells of Gratitude, Love, and Fortune for Thanksgiving

The Boogey Chronicles: A Journal of Nightly Encounters and Shadowy Secrets

The 12 Days of Financial Freedom: A Step-by-Step Christmas Countdown to Transform Your Finances

Sigil of the Eternal Spiral Blank Journal

A Christmas Feast: Timeless Recipes for Every Meal

Cosmic Sales: The Astrological Guide to Black Friday Shopping
Legends of the Corn Mother and Other Harvest Myths
Whispers of the Harvest: The Corn Mother's Journal
The Evergreen Spellbook
The Doctor Meets the Boogeyman
The White Witch of Rose Hall's SpellBook
The Gingerbread Golem's Shadow: A Study in Sweet Darkness
The Gingerbread Golem Codex: An Academic Exploration of Sweet Myths
The Gingerbread Golem Grimoire: Sweet Magicks and Spells for the Festive Witch
The Curse of the Gingerbread Golem
10-minute Christmas Crafts for kids
<u>Christmas Crisis Solutions: The Ultimate Last-Minute Survival Guide</u>
Gingerbread Golem Recipes: Holiday Treats with a Magical Twist
The Infinite Key: Unlocking Mystical Secrets of the Ages
Enchanted Yule: A Wiccan and Pagan Guide to a Magical and Memorable Season
Dinosaurs of Power: Unlocking Ancient Magick
Astro-Dinos: The Cosmic Guide to Prehistoric Wisdom
Gallifrey's Yule Logs: A Festive Doctor Who Cookbook
The Dino Grimoire: Secrets of Prehistoric Magick
The Gift They Never Knew They Needed
The Gingerbread Golem's Culinary Alchemy: Enchanting Recipes for a Sweetly Dark Feast
A Time Lord Christmas: Holiday Adventures with the Doctor
Krampusproofing Your Home: Defensive Strategies for Yule
Silent Frights: A Collection of Christmas Creepypastas to Chill Your Bones
Santa Raptor's Jolly Carnage: A Dino-Claus Christmas Tale
Prehistoric Palettes: A Dino Wicca Coloring Journey
The Christmas Wishkeeper Chronicles

The Micro-Mastery Method: Transform Your Skills in Just Minutes a Day

Reclaiming Time: How to Live More by Doing Less

Chronovore: The Eternal Nexus

The Mind Reset: Unlocking Your Inner Peace in a Chaotic World

Confidence Code: Building Unshakable Self-Belief

Baby the Vampire Terrier

Baby the Vampire Terrier's Christmas Adventure

Celestial Streams: The Content Creator's Astrology Manual

The Wealth Whisperer: Unlocking Abundance with Everyday Actions

The Energy Equation: Maximize Your Output Without Burning Out

If you want solar for your home go here: https://www.harborsolar.live/apophisenterprises/

Get Some Tarot cards: https://www.makeplayingcards.com/sell/apophis-occult-shop

<u>Get   some   shirts: https://www.bonfire.com/store/apophis-shirt-emporium/</u>

<u>Instagrams:</u>
@apophis_enterprises,
@apophisbookemporium,
@apophisscardshop
Twitter: @apophisenterpr1
 Tiktok:@apophisenterprise
Youtube: @sg1fan23477, @FiresideRetreatKingdom
Hive: @sg1fan23477
CheeLee: @SG1fan23477

Podcast: Apophis Chat Zone: https://open.spotify.com/show/
5zXbrCLEV2xzCp8ybrfHsk?si=fb4d4fdbdce44dec

Newsletter: https://apophiss-newsletter-27c897.beehiiv.com/

If you want to support me or see posts of other projects that I have come over to: **buymeacoffee.com/mpetchinskg**
I post there daily several times a day

Get your Dinowicca or Christmas themed digital products, especially Santa Raptor songs and other musics. Here: **https://sg1fan23477.gumroad.com**

Apophis Yuletide Digital has not only digital Christmas items, but it will have all things with Dinowicca as well as other Digital products.